GET
FRESH BOOKS

Praise for WHEN THE TREES FINALLY TESTIY

Bonita Lee Penn's words in *When the Trees Finally Testify* are at once a sharp-edged sword and a sweet balm of healing for what aches. Her poetry speaks to histories that beckon us to remember and reclaim our truths. Bonita marries rage with the divine and gives new life to poetics.

- DuEwa Frazier, poet & author of *Goddess Under the Bridge: Poems,* producer/host of *Nerdacity*

Poets have the impossible task of balancing their mind and spirit, their duende, and all of the histories around them into lyric movements of inspiration and protest. Most poets can't manage all their disparate obligations, but as readers will soon recognize, Bonita Penn can and does in her stunning new collection *When the Trees Finally Testify.* Only a poet as deft as Penn can call out the American traditions of violence and oppression with the same strength and clarity as she praises Black generosity and love. *When the Trees Finally Testify* is a book of texture and capaciousness like none I've read before. These are poems of awareness and witness. These are poems of resistance and bounty.

- Adrian Matejka, Editor, *Poetry* magazine

In *When the Trees Finally Testify* by Bonita Lee Penn, do not be alarmed after reading the first 20 or so pages. That ringing in your dome is language doing the difficult-beautiful work, the unafraid-heavy-lifting that "testifies" on behalf of the Black experience. By the time you arrive in *media res* please understand you are being old-skooled-schooled by a poet standing on history's broad shoulders as well as its literary figures that helped craft a "tradition." In the words of Amiri Baraka, these are live words of the hip world. No cut cards held here. These poems will cloak you in love or send you out into these streets with a placard demanding change. There is depth and brevity to this beautiful collection. Consider *When the Trees Finally Testify,* as Gwendolyn Brooks might articulate, "a report from the inside." What a tremendous achievement.

- Randall Horton, author, *#289-128: Poems*

Get Fresh Publishing, A Non-Profit Corp.
PO Box 901
Union, NJ 07083

www.gfbpublishing.org

ISBN: 9798218359355

Library of Congress Control Number: 2024933938
Cover, layout, typesetting, and design:
Anny Caba
AnnyCaba.com

Cover Image by Autumn N. Woodland

This book was typeset in Heavitas, Avenir Next, and Times New Roman

Contents

WHEN THE TREES FINALLY TESTIFY

by Bonita Lee Penn

we can't talk about freedom

without talking about the hulls

without talking about the chains

without talking about the blood

without talking about the screams

without talking about the deaths

without talking about the rebirth

without talking about the possibilities

-unknown

the dismemberment of remembrance

if you find a tree with the rope, or some piece intact / enough to test
the age, type, and where it was made. / on that rope, tested / some secret
type of test / that alternative truth type test. / perhaps. / if the rope still
has trace of dna of a negro man / negro woman / negro child / animal /
they can test that speck of blood. / not, the ancestry spit test / you /
know / the tall tale fact tests / you know to make sure the outcome / is
paid insurance. / wait / they would also need photos of the lynching /
color snapshots preferred / different advantage points / cause, you
know / we all look alike / even dead / hung from branches. / photos
to be used / as confirmation / if / it was an animal / black child / black
woman / black man. / you do know / after the burning / we all look
alike / smell like / we-done. / the photo would need to be tested / for
age / make of paper / to be sure / of its / lies. / a fabrication of a
disgruntle enslaved, jim crow'd person or persons. / confirm the date
written on the front of the photo / in bad hand writing / smears of
chicken grease. / if this did take place / on this date / this time / in this
place / and if it was indeed a black woman / black child / black
man / animal. / then the need of the dna of the lynchers / to confirm /
indeed / it was white men / boys / women / affiliated with this /
said / lynching. / plus, the trial manuscripts or police non-report / to
prove the man, black / woman, black / animal / child, black / was
innocent of their / subsequent death / or well deserving / to be hung
by the neck / till dead / till the urine stopped / till bowels empty /
shitless / screams / ceased. / but wait / they would need the hour /
minute / screams started / to the last scream / to measure / lynching's
labor was / or not / cruel punishment / cause black folks don't feel
pain / cause white folks ain't that type of evil / just to kill / for pleasure
/ or to kill for the crime of not being white / crimes of being in the wake
of blackness. / to believe / they / lynched / on a regular / still no
reparations. / did they test the ashes / in the gas chambers of auschwitz /
did they test the stale air / for zyklon b / yet those survivors / received
their / reparations.

Lynched Ghosts' Song #2: Trees in Snow

thick plot of skeletal bodied trees   maybe a hundred or so
stand   some as though knees hurt   naked within
         their natural collective – platoon.

fills this country dead-end road's wide snowy plateau   dark bark
a heavy burden   petrified memories   those nightmarish filled
     wails as they rose   out of burnt throats of strange fruits, hanging . . .

branches exposed   stretched up-ward   chants towards the heavens
forgiveness prayers
                    forgive me for I know not what they were going to do

bodies rooted in a rotted history   some brood in sins of others
branches militarized   solitary soldiers   carry out commands

to carry then break the weight

imagine a field of naked trees dressed in black funeral flesh.

          take me to the water, take me to the water, take me to the
                    water to be sanctified

beneath partially buried rooted trunk roots, filled with empty
holes   leak desperate pleas, dying dead weight too
heavy to bear

a tree falls in the snow   its pain cushioned by earth

its last breath prays to be taken back to dust
ashes   to ashes
blood of their blood.

Beware of the Quiet Ones,
As We Are Our Daily Bread

we are not broken
we are not hurt
we are not all bitter
or angry, or shallow
or nonexistent

the sun shines on our skin
and our lips part in smiles
all day, and night, even in
our sleep we smile and breathe

we are not rude and fight in clubs
with fists and fingers that grab
weave and hair, and knot it around
fingers to tug and toss to stomp
in the curve of curbs, or to smash
into the horizontal of walls
we are not those fists that grab knives
and bottles to be smashed then jagged
razor edges to be used to slice flesh

the moon cools our skin
and our lips part in songs, in
prayers, in chants to celebrate
the beauty of love, of earthly
gardens that bloom underneath
our feet as we walk, as we skip,
and we dance and the moon cools
our skin and our lips part

and our razor-cut teeth stained
with blood and earthly rewards
speak your name

A Political Act, Absolutely

An impi body of African women
in America.
Regiments of hips and waist
beads.

A freed movement, an
oscillation
of what seems to be an
all-out assault on
all spaces   white   spaces.

Tsunamis are we   when we
breathe, when we
breathe, when   we walk on,
bye.

When our mouths   open
ALL   OUT   LOUD.

All loud, fierce, fearless, the way Angela
        said the word absolutely
with a smile, we know . . .

When we   speak, it is water-
falls up & out   between
gapped teeth, like mercury
then gathers itself up
and we   speak-

loudly   *absolutely*
we do, motherfuckers.

The scent of our sweat collects
at our feet   creates pools
of mysteriously ancient things.

Of some things threatening,
as though we could bend metal
bars, shape-shift, deflect bullets
and bullshit, dance on water, or
take off in flight.

How Some Folks Get to Space Without a Rocket

with the sound of the currents above
my hair naturally tangles and hangs
and flies upward with the wind and
upwards with my laughter, as the sun
is always there to greet each morning
and the moon embraces me to dream
and sleep and create. if I am blessed with
rain, it is my father's voice calling out
my name. it is where my mind goes when
it needs to breathe, when it tires of
survival mode, and my flesh remembers
it is beautiful, it is a living life, and it is able
to reach out and touch the sky.

What Powers Us

words do not decipher in her dreams
nor do they guide to the chant's manifestation
or the ceremonial dress
if she is to be bathed in white
or move in her own nakedness

should her hair be tied in green vines
or shells dangle from her neck, in music
around her waist and ankles

she does not yet know what role herb healers play

or how to dance the way she is to dance
should her hips move, in what ways
should her body shake, in what ways

the words have yet to manifest in her dreams
they exist, but yet to present
as she looks toward sky with praises
she knows its existence understands her

should her hands clap or does she kneel and
beat the trunk of great trees

should her feet stomp or prance lightly

should people circle her, linked fingers
or stand at arm's length, should they walk
towards her, or lift their arms as she dances
will they fall back as she turns and lifts her
arms to the sky

will the people sing after her lead
or will their songs guide her chants
in her dreams, she wonders

should her voice bellow from the ocean's
floor, should her voice rise and crash like
waves guided by the moon's path

should the people catch her as she flails
will they pretend to hold her ankles
when she takes off in flight

in her dreams she is a healer
the moon is not her path but
her song

Prelude to the Search, Discovery, Destruction, and Then the Reconstruction of Black Women

i place myself in a search engine myself is thrown back regurgitated
a parody stew fragmented cartoonish lumps distorted and mythical
de-boned images a narrative framed flesh seen through the engine's
eyes this is how sight is programmed.

in search of hairstyles   black women's hairstyles images appear wow!
images of me's scroll down once more scroll down white women appear
in the search for myself what is the search engine telling me of beauty
not enough Black women have beautiful hairstyles here the search
engine shoves these try these beauties.

concise with search request narrow, narrower, narrowest only black
women only black women still they invade the sanctuary of black
women only spaces get this they are adorned in cornrows flowing
ribbons of bleached wispy locs where oh where, did we go?

let's play the game insert— black men sing love songs to black women
search engine says says bitch media but there are 55 songs by black
women black girls rock 13 hip-hop songs 15 classic songs every black
girl knows the words is this how the engine narrows down the black
man out of our equation it is lonely out here in this exiled space of
only for black women requests.

*gurl you know we only playing, laughs the search engine, come on
back, black sheba, try again.*

old school search, through top heavy shelves with 12 x12 cardstock
envelopes vinyl filled sleeves this search does not require catch words
manual fingers work to flip from one to the next until you find— the
makings of you makings of— black women place it on the turntable the
sharp stylus gently drops a successful search Curtis Mayfield wow!
black women love his song a black woman's love song our humanity

Disclaimer:
Not all search engines will display the images and phrases used.
This particular search was conducted years ago. Hopefully, since
then the engine has been recalibrated.

Algorithms of the Black Feminine Body, a choreopoem

> *Add a little sugar, honeysuckle*
> *and a great expression of happiness*
> *boy you couldn't miss*
> *with a dozen roses*
> *such will astound you*
> *the joy of children laughing around you*
> *these are the makings of you*
> *it is true, the makings of you*
> —Curtis Mayfield

The Black woman's
     opinion is a political battleground.
[why do you say, how we make, being visible, invisible,
show the way, white woman's opinion, black men's opinion as to]

The Black woman's
     hair is a political battleground.
[to know, identity, natural bias, confess, the caucasian guide, straightened,
never told, what's up with, the politics of, speak about]

The Black woman's
     garments are political battlegrounds.
[church suits, modest apparel, brands, trends, ideas, African, unique, wigs,
black and white, especially yours, style images, need to be]

The Black woman's
     melody is a political battleground.
[get over it, living well, catchin' hell, social stress, hood,
stop apologizing, guide to, reviews, outdoor research, pros and cons]

The Black woman's
     poetry is a political battleground.
[15 black women poets and 7 more dope black women,
poets, to celebrate, to read, to teach, keep you calm, cool]

The Black woman's
*[question of survival, discursive space of feminism and black,
portrait of being a, struggle for empowerment, studies in women]*
    predicament is a political battleground.

The Black woman's
    ovulation is a political battleground.
*[fertility, struggle, to know, secret to, 7 signs, vaginal discharge,
menopause, what to know, captured on film, booty call, detect]*

The Black woman's
    saga is a political battleground.
*[social media, scanned from the book, swiping left, images for, black stiletto,
a sci-fi take, hypersexualization, obsession with, scumball saga]*

The Black woman's
    eating habits are political battlegrounds.
*[... and intention to change, slave food, behaviors and portion sizes,
self-efficacy, sustainable, silent struggle, eating disorders, behavior, sizes]*

The Black woman's
    BMI is a political battleground.
*[Black Health Matters, does it apply, black girls run, perception,
healthy thought, waist may be bigger, BlackDoctor, scale broken]*

and my sisters of the opinionate formation, rise—
#MeToo \ #SayHerName \ #BringBackOurGirls
#BlackGirlMagic \ #BlkWomenSyllabus \ #StayMadAbby \ #GrowingUpBlack \
#BlackLivesMatter \ #TakeItDown
#MissingDCGirls \ #BlackWomenDidThat \ #CareFreeBlackGirl \ #AssaultAtSpringValley
\ #IfIDieInPoliceCustody—Amen.

and the kitchen hair of my sisters spring loose and sings, Rise—
coils, bantu knots, cornrow designs, ghana braids, kinky twists,
locs, flat-ironed, blow-out, afro, plaits, tapered, shaved sides,
peacock feathers of colors, sew-in, clip-in, variety of textures
—Amen.

The Black woman's
      visions are political battlegrounds.
*[future creators, rich, varied, being with, imperative, happy, manifest,
mindset, power, mission, ventures, mule of the world, blueprint]*

The Black woman's
*[breast cancer, 13 quotes, shop for, self-preservation, a question of,
cancer, unspeakable burden, how to not die, the lowest, toxic white]*
      survival is a political battleground.

The Black woman's
*[no accident, 75,000 Black Girls and Women, calls, America's problem,
no one seems to care, spark outrage, national issue of . . .]*
      disappearance— is a political battleground.

Freedom is the Black woman's
*[body become her own, abolitionists, formerly enslaved, role in slavery,
human dignity, limits of, let it shine, fighters, agency, activists]*
      political battleground.

The Black woman's
      pleasure is a political battleground.
*[God, guilt, sexual, divine, how-to-please, fetishized racism, porn,
love letter, multiple, feminist genealogy, to explore that in bedroom]*

The Black woman's
*[what we get wrong, no need to reclaim, liberation, objectification,
so dangerous, always been overpoliced, longing to tell, unapologetically, study]*
      sexuality is a political battleground.

The Black woman's
>   **allegiance** is a political battleground.
[manifesto, leaders refuse, alliance, PhD, Nate Parker, status, domestic, dating,
avant-garde, expelled, confront the West, loyalist, absolute love of]

The Black woman's
>   **revolution** is a political battleground.
[say it loud, act that defies, is God, activist, mindset,
major roles, she has risen, panther, we wanted a, extraordinary]

The Black woman's
>   **"roll-of-her-eyes"** is a political battleground.
[all of us, divas, kinda-scary, secret language, civil rights,
round-the-world, whenever, chatting with, stock photos, secret language]

The Black woman's
>   **shit** is a political battleground.
[realizing, will my son, hate crimes, I-don't-give, superpowers,
cringe-worthy, displaced, don't-owe-you, slams, white woman attacks]

Look in the mirror & what do we see?

and my sisters who swing words like switchblades, rise—
Maxine Waters, Ntozake Shange, Sonia Sanchez, Winnie Mandela,
Chimamanda Ngozi Adichie, Audre Lorde, Jessica Care Moore,
Wangari Maathai, Anna Tibaijuka, Toni Morrison, Alice Walker,
Angela Davis, bell hooks, Ursula Rucker, Joy Kmt,
Nana Sekyiamah, Staceyann Chin, Warsan Shire—Amen.

the hands of my sisters covered in glue/paint/clay/indigo/wood/ash, rise—
Bettye Saar, Carrie Mae Weems, Kara Walker, Krista Franklin, Bisa Butler, LaVerne
Kemp, Mary Sibande, Tamara Natalie Madden, Alisha Wormsley,
Elizabeth Catlett, Faith Ringgold, Dindga McCannon, Howardena Pindell, Barbara
Chase-Riboud, Simone Leigh, Mickalene Thomas, Samella Lewis, Njideka Akinjuli
Crosby, Wangechi Mutu, Aïda Muluneh—Amen.

The Black woman's
      intelligence is a political battleground.
*[notes on, don't insult, successful, report confirms, perceiving, advise to
why google thought, propelling, covert war, why, protest, portrait, spies]*

The Black woman's
      flight-or-fight is a political battleground.
*[men respond, while anxious, poor health, hypothesis, fly girls, strength,
against white woman's feet, sent to back, tend and befriend]*

The Black woman's
      DNA is a political battleground.
*[claim about existence, Eve gene, Henrietta Lacks, mitochondrial, test reveals,
changed modern medicine, race in science, cells were priceless, source]*

The Black woman's
      weaponry-of-language is a political battleground.
*[amazon warriors, loaded weapon, resistance, sign language, lethal, woman, ways
transformed conditioned silence, use and abuse, Afrofuturism, new ways, speaking]*

The Black woman's
      complexions are political battlegrounds.
*[dark, sick, light, healthy, truths, images, not-just-about, beautiful,
get real, even the tone, what-does-it-mean, secret]*

The Black woman's
*[what are you doing, silver, skin-blackening, toxicity, environment, madness,
rouge Dior, message, the costume, sassy, deeper than death, hurricane]*
      375-distinct-metals-which-make-up-her-body
      is a political battleground.

The Black woman's
*[spoken word, death of, extraordinary, last-will, images for, Sojourner's,
Sunday inspirations, also are the, telling, GIFs, like a dream]*
      smile is a political battleground.

The Black woman's
[disdain, doesn't stop, disrespected, response, towards, war on, damaged, appeals,
die in childbirth, interracial, dissed, now disappeared, defies the rules]
      contempt is always a political battleground.

The Black woman's
      artistic skills are political battlegrounds.
[Simone Biles vs. the racists, rarest skills, nude, woman who insists,
blkwomenart, theatre, B.R.A.V.E., reimagined, black woman and white man ideas]

The Black woman's
      familiarity is a political battleground.
[in the bedroom, plight of, burden, disrespect, you mad, commodifying,
not-your-sista, justification for, honor, low-on-funds, privilege]

Look in the mirror & what do we see?

the humming voices of my sisters who wade in the waters, rise—
Nina Simone, Billie Holiday, Sweet Honey in the Rock, Mariam Maekba, Aretha
Franklin, Fatoumata Diawara, India Arie, Tracey Chapman. Thandiswa Mazwai,
Roberta Flack, Queen Latifah, Lauryn Hill, Celia Cruz, Mavis Staples, Meshell
Ndegeocello, Dobet Gnahoré, Lira—Amen.

the Sayers of names, will not let our sister voices disappear, rise—
Alberta Spruill, Miriam Care, Korryn Gaines, Rekia Boyd, Tanisha Anderson, Yvette
Smith, Shelly Frey, Darnisha Harris, Malissa Williams, Alesia Thomas, Shantel Davis,
Shereese Francis, Tarika Wilson, Kathryn Johnston, Aiyana Stanley-Jones, Kendra James,
Olivia Gilbert, Kimberly Waller, Delicious Jones, Tina Crawford, Lauren Williams, Susan
Sidney, Cheralyn Sabatasso, Keiauna Davis—Amen.

The Black woman's
      darkness is a political battleground.
[queen of, celebrates being, bullied for, told to, bleach her,
unbearable of, end of, stunningly, Nubian planet, tired of hearing]

The Black woman's
> **empathy** is a political battleground.

*[white tears, limit, intersectionality, lemonade, permission, not enough, pass for,
born unapologetic, multicolor, selective, founded, don't feel like, bitchy, costs]*

The Black woman's
> **prayer-circles** are political battlegrounds.

*[healing, medicine, awakening, ancient methods, collectibles, fierce, tell your story,
clip art, circle guidelines, dreams, high vibe yoga, lives of]*

The Black woman's
> **butter-pound-cake** is a political battleground.

*[Perfect, Old School, Grandpa's, Million Dollar, Pantry, Mama's 7UP, Luscious
Divas Can Cook, Rum Cake, Deep South Dish, Easy]*

The Black woman's

*[smudges, reveal, lightning powder, dusting for, bodily traces, embodied memories,
lack scientific basis, legal certainty, disappearing, changes and verifications, left]*
> **fingerprints—her DNA lineage** is a political battleground.

The Black woman's
> **breath** is a political battleground.

*[silent-killer, speaks volumes, be here, memory, intimacy, transformative, journey
never taken, flowers too, women of color healing retreats, take]*

The Black woman's
> **lifted-brow** is a political battleground.

*[balancing-acts, the master, gone daddy gone, Aboriginal women warriors,
in the name of, the thought, conversation with Mahogany L.]*

The Black woman's
> **stance** is a political battleground.

*[defense, collection, best-selling, uncommon, take aim, world black chat,
to pimp, defense league, taking aim, uncommon super, and crime]*

The Black woman's
        children are political battlegrounds.
*[fearless, leaders, highest rate, unequal, state of, mothering, understanding,
books about, lag behind, two white babies, out-of-wedlock]*

The Black woman's
        clapbacks are political battlegrounds.
*[8 best, owning her anger, twitter erased, standing ovation, epic,
why i'm here, black mirror, news anchor's, diamond and silk]*

Look in the mirror & what do we see?

the Sayers of names, who speak loud for our sisters who said "no," rise—
Tiarah Poyau, Janese Talton-Jackson, Cherica Adams, Jessica Hampton, Nokuthula
Thashe, Nova Henry, Mary Spears, Kasandra Perkins, LaVena Johnson, April Jace,
Julia Martin—Amen.

we gather at banks of rivers, ocean shores, under trees, and we dance—
Moribayasa, from the Malinke people in Guinea. Dance done by women who have
overcome great adversity. The woman starts the dance wearing old and ragged clothes.
Accompanied by musicians, she circles the village several times, singing and dancing.
The women of the village follow her and also sing. The woman then changes her clothes
and buries her old clothes in a special area.

The Black woman's
        gardens are political battlegrounds.
*[destroyed in the hood, in search of, colored woman, telling,
smiling, take a look at, redefining, song of songs, roses]*

The Black woman's
*[soul talk, spiritual resistance, woman's curse, free, false, anomaly, embracing,
God is curvy, guide to healthy living, spiritual resistance for]*
        spirit is a political battleground.

The Black woman's
      menopause is a political battleground.
*[different view, onset, endure, perceptions of, hormone, alliance, symptoms last,
with heart, worse for, use of hormone, four different patterns]*

The Black woman's
      "no" is a political battleground.
*[will not be returning, reflections on roles, Black wonder woman?,
liberations, herstory, Shirley Chisholm, truths of dating, woman mayor, cocoons]*

The Black woman's
*[Mmmmm, you don't know the words, angry woman, an anthology,
what are you doing here, reprogramming that God code, mysterious]*
      hum is a political battleground.

The Black woman's
      Wild Seed is a political battleground.
*[what is, who owns, thrives, illustrates, analysis, Octavia Butler, scholar,
interview, of the select, reclaims humanism, Untitled, Queer, Black Code]*

The Black woman's
      adoration is a political battleground.
*[of whiteness, regarding Africa, Negritude, crisis of, community of slaves,
myth, freeing one's mind, and eroticism, body types, last frontier]*

The Black woman's
      thoughtpatterns are political battlegrounds.
*[colonizing, female bodies, wealthy mindset, sadness, collective, break free, worth,
significance, speaking in tongues, embracing, self-recovery, yams, ready, willing]*

The Black woman's **sustainability** is a political battlefield.
*[our communities, quest for, hair products, we all we got,
emergent, moving our, drawing parallels, possibilities for global, our favorite]*

The Black woman's
[an Anthology, Mothers, Medicine, Morality, Legend long ago, beauty of,
American crossroads, my eyes filled with oceans, African dance, remix]
Moribayasa is a political battleground.

The love of all mankind
should reflect some sign of these words
I've tried to recite
they're close but not quite
almost impossible to do
reciting the makings of you
—Curtis Mayfield "The Makings of You"

Don't Get It Twisted

cause we be allowed to be fine like this
eyelashes glued and flutters like wings
        of an albatross
cool our bodies as we walk the walk in 24/7 summer heat
        that is our blood.

we walk in formation in sky blue, ripped, shredded skinny jeans
        and our titties pressed tight as nipples sing cause we
                pretty and pretty sings.

we are baddd, this what we got from those like
        Carolyn Rodgers,
        Sonia Sanchez, baddd m.f. truth-saying sisters.

that symbolic glitter of our magic, that does not quietly fall
        to the ground, we sound more like hydrogen bombs.

cause we loud and we pretty.

and our eyelashes flutter like death's ashes blow in the wind.
        we here, and everywhere.

Courageous Acts of Being

belts   of ocean slap   against rocks   then
roll gently to fill empty spaces

if living breaths of Black women's skin, were
sounds   of implosions from   in in inside

& hummingbirds in veiled   trees
peck   peck   pecker-wood   pecks

if being Black skin were   sounds
of   destruction

crows black   and brilliant   and blaring
fly and nest on live wires, wait to
let   shit—drop

if Black women's   skin were   sounds
crackling pig skin, burnt scraps   drown
in the bottom of the caste-iron   of used
oil

half-drunk gin bottles   flung against table's edge
and flesh rips, spurts of blood   pelt the floor
if dying Black skin were   sounds, and

skin   so silent it whimpers, and its claws were
hurricanes (katrina, her sisters, and em) shatter
the hate of the earth's crust, hate that cries loud
and hard to silent Black women's breaths

if the breath of Black women were   sounds, were
rumbles, were thunder, were heels that sidestep
cracked sidewalks (step on the crack breaks ya
momma's back)

if the breath of Black women were side steps
whoa, watch us   step

Hurried She Came

as hurricanes
as tsunamis
as earthquakes
as volcanos.

she is an eruption
a path of destruction
that interrupts the normalcy
of dysfunctional societies.

the sacrifice of many
meant to wake up those
few who came to, and did
wreak havoc on her body.

a body of water, of earth
of trees, of birds, of fish.

of sun, of moon, both sides of her.
under her skirt of clouds, of stars,
of winds,

her breath of fresh air, releases
flowers, plant scents of greenery.
the after scent of rain, the comfort
of warm winds, the chill of cool nights.

she comes as wet flood from the sea
to the lakes, to the rivers, to the creeks,
and the seeds of the ancestors swim
up her thighs.

Being a Single Black Woman, on a Moonlit Night, When Lightning Rides Thunder Bareback

is all that is seen / piano keys dance / click and clack / kick, slides cross empty palms / snap of heels on concrete stairs / ledge unsteady as hot wind hurries through a field / cane field / flames chase / sweet douse of tears that stopped crawling out lids / wet love potions / mixture of red clay / mother's land soil that sleeps on forest floors / selected winds that surf tall field grass and hollers between cotton barbs / drops of sun rays burnt through levees / scrapple of vodou watchwords / drowns the battlegrounds drawn in the / silence of black men. / deep- red bone legit ligaments disconnect / but inner connectivity to what ails lonely thighs / tightly loose and ready to jump / how wide. / rainbow's toss sprinkles to douse her flames / speaks of nefertiti and sheba's yoruba's second cousin who spoke ibo / and dressed in mudcloth / and carried a nguni shield but spoke xhosa / this black male smoke screen all over the place / as her emotions / as she fidgets in her emptiness / in thoughts of a man who may speak ibo / xhosa / blackened english / and who holds his head high for the love of clean water and black women / whose songs are wild hurricanes.

Not About To

Black women not about to apologize for
       breathing
for being
       born
for
       laughing loud
for
       razor blades hidden between cheek and gums
for
       carrying hot sauce in our purses
       carrying mace
for
       loving to dance
       in any place
for
       braiding our hair
for
       coloring our hair blonde
for
       wearing headwraps
for
       not inviting you to the cookouts
       or to our retreats

every morning a foot is looking for my neck

roll porcupine tight
squeeze in between tight
out the way spaces.

disappear.

told us to carry the burdens:
nasty, dirty, big booty, black
and racist, big-hips and bitter
feminist, revolutionist pissed
poet. shadow of an evil-eyed
animal. not woman enough
to be loved, a wife, never a
mother. one of those uppity,
mixed-up bitches, one of them
too educated m.f.'ers. ignore her.
screw her. throw her away.

shove her in a dark corner. evict
her from her own box. bury her.
silence her. erase her humanity in
stained exotic pornopostcards,
dressed in veils, hijab or bananas.

the world yells and tells us to be
a chameleon. to blend, to press our-
selves into the recesses, into shadows
of our skin. to lay low, to be silent, to
shrink. disappear.

**You Laughed at My Wails and Whining, Then I Showed You
My Storm and Slapped the Shit Out of You**

Something about the power of wind, you
sense its arrival before you feel it, if your
mouth opens in awe, she will tease
you with her dust as she lifts her skirt
and shakes it and performs the whirl
of wind dance.

An invisible knock at a door, or sounds
of pebbles flung at a window, as the
wind dashes and slaps the lids off filled
garbage cans, and the lids chase her
down the street playing a tin tune to
seduce her as they beg to come along.

or the sisterhood of leaves tries to
break free of the branch, to break in
to your 2nd-floor bedroom window.

or when you run in your attempt to
outrun her storm that comes down
like the residue of firecrackers, but
still filled with the flames, and slaps
you in the face with grits of hail,
and blindfolds you with sisterleaves
who broke free.

here you come walking through a field
of tall grass, she comes at you
from underneath the roots and rubs
against your flesh like a taffeta dress,
rough and noisy, and your legs begin to itch.

call to her, the wind, the beauty as you
greet the ocean rush, it fills the emptiness
between your thighs and plays with
clit or buoyant balls. you cannot help
but surrender a smile, as she is warmth.

you think, yes, this is what freedom feels
like, warmth and the ability to fly, but you
swim, and the wind is what moves the
current as it slaps your chest and you
run back to the anchor of the shore.

wind can and will tear trees out of their
mother's womb, did you read how they
watched the walls waiting for God to
save them, but the Seminoles already
told them she was coming, and they
should leave, as she was dressed in her
war paint ready to bitch-slap the world.

the bayou is her favorite place to do
too much, yes she does too much, the
whirl, wail of her wind moves not like
a ghost smoothly through walls, but a
fury that breaks all barricades, and she
whirls so fast, she becomes nauseated
and vomits mississippi waters, splitting
levees, damns, and sand-filled bags.

the mouth of her anger sings out and
raises the dead, whips down the living.

blow, blowing, blown
drown and them done drowned.

and I was born on a darkened night
when the sky was so black it was indigo
invisible, an infinity globe of darkness,
as though the world was coming to its end
or a new beginning was being created, they
call this the wind, the storm, the hurricane,
before birth I was nothing more than a
wail and a whine.

Testify, Testify, Testify, I Will

Ntozake, Ntozake
Ntozake, Ntozake

n here

She slowly strokes her fingers over her throat

Ntozake
Ntozake

n here

She slowly presses the palm of her hand and circles her breast/heart

Ntozake
Ntozake

n here

She purposely slides her hands over her hips and smiles

Ntozake, Ntozake
Ntozake, Ntozake

n here

She raises her eyebrow, puts out her hand and marks her personal space

all black girls
break it down
Ntozake

get down, get down   *She does the get down*
get down, get down
get down, get down

when nappy edges   *She stops the antics*
said "she tried it"
when nappy edges
said "no" to edge control

black bodies
they tried it
black bodies
to be controlled
they keep trying it
Ntozake
Ntozake

they tried it
break us free
Ntozake
broke us free

lover of warriors
Toussaint Louverture
broke us free
to dance to willie colon
to jam to jimi hendrix
to get freed with bob marley

Ntozake
broke us free to dance
the way we want to dance

i do not need to shake my hips
or drop crystals from my pussy
or pull a pulitzer poem from my
my crotch, for you to know
to know i know
believe
Ntozake
broke us free

who wants to live in the world
when we own the universe the
world ain't neva been big enough
for free black women, now we
living in the universe, the world
ain't good enough when we
done tasted the desert, the ocean
the mountains, the skies

i do not need to walk on water
Ntozake
Ntozake
our favorite word is no
after an evening of sex
turned to rape and rape
not rough sex, sex turned
to rape and rape

in my head i danced, i danced
he forced himself inside me
as i danced in my head with
my dahomey mothers, and
sanite bélair gathered round me
and danced shouted viv libète
as he tried to take my magic and
but all he took was—an empty
space
i walked away . . .
Ntozake

n here *[hands caress my head]*
Ntozake
n here this colored girl
walked away . . .
this colored girl still
alive

freedom is to walk
at night, to stand in
the dusk as the sun
turns the sky shades
of honey buttered toast
freedom is to walk
at night, alone, to
stand at a bus, at a train
stop, and be safe

Ntozake, Ntozake
Ntozake, Ntozake
n here, n here, n here
n till all women are free

She lays down to rest.

Mary, Don't You Weep, Tell Martha Not to Moan

Sister
it is hard to live here
aqui tambem
irmã.

To be a woman here is dangerous
é perigoso para mulheres
aqui também irmã

Is there no God?   No protection?
Não há Deus, não há proteção
No God   sister   but prayer . . .
        oração
for my children
para meus filhos
        for our children, sister.

Prayers for me
orações por mim
for all of us   sister . . .

for our country. *para o nosso país*
    where is your country? *onde é seu país?*
Our country? *nosso país?*

No country   For women
Sisters.   No country.

Nenhum país.   Para as mulheres.
Sisters.   No country.

**For Marielle Franco, a Black activist who campaigned fearlessly against gender-based violence and police violence against Blacks in Brasil.*

Psalms for My Sisters' Warrior Shields

> *yea thou I walk through the valley of the shadow*
> —Psalms 23:4

found in our mothers', mothers', mothers' mouths, tongues hot grill
comb marks doused in corn liquor. signs of endless days, combat
against darkness's confessional vicious clutch. daughters, sisters,
mothers, providers of protection, soars on heaven's winds. shields
against ghost ropes' death knots; drips of kinship. regurgitate labels,
press against them kitchens, claim resistant fingers—oracles. in laundry
rooms meant to drown dreams. women gatherers conjure at the base of
baobab trees, roots of our mothers' graves, of their sisters' graves,
of our daughters' graves, and we give birth—to fire.

We Wanted a Revolution

Am   I
the   only
 one

who dreams of a revolution?

Of black   brown folks
even those   in-between folks

Even those whose native land is not of
African soil,
But still whose skins are shadow hues

Even those whose bloodlines were drowned
in a diluted gene pool

Am   I
the only
 one

who dreams of falling asleep
to the drums of the Maroons
          and
wakes to the shake of the earth's
echoes
 Zulu
 Zulu

As we all—in our burnished skins—
march in unison over this country
over the seas.

In wide-world gush of unison
knock down cement walls
rush checkpoints
fill hidden tunnels in Palestine.

Climb the hills of the favelas in Brasil.

Through the Townships of South Africa.

The inequities of Cuba.

Feet trample rabbit fences in Australia.
Give voice to those who suffer in silence in New Zealand
Ka Mate
Ka Mate ka okra.

We all were once warriors.

Am I
the only
one

who dreams of being free.

The Eleventh-Hour Manifesto
after Dareen Tatour's "I Will Not Leave My Country"

you do not
you do not
you do not
you don't
want to hear
the words
the words
do not want
to hear
listen to the
flesh
ree leased
ree leased
and rock
rock
the mothers
hold onto
dead bodies
like an award

this country
this country
celebrates war
always celebrates
its wars
even the declared
war on war on
let my people go
we can call it the
100 year war, but
it is the 300+ year
it is the everyday war
this country

this country
and its wars
and its hate
and its hate
and its wars
and its hate
this country
its ignorance
this country
this country
tis of thee

where we live
where we can not
breathe
where we can not
jog
where we can   not
wear our natural
hair, speak our
natural language

this country
this country
filled with poems
that side eye of #saytheirname
that shade of #blacklivesmatter
this country filled
with dark matter
this country
our country
this   is   my country

Byproduct of the Body's Defensive Wall

spaces
like the
silence
between
the

trigger
being
pulled, the
bullet
slides

out the
chamber,
razors
its way
through

tissue.

Testification of the Trees
> *There is a Tree More Ancient than Eden**

The mossy oak—will be the star witness when those who did the
   lynchings
whose time has come to stand at the entrance of those pearly gates.

The Lawd— will raise his right hand and question,
> *who will testify of this man's goodwill*
> *of this man's humanity?*

The wind will rip thru the moss and the tree more ancient than Eden
will stand to testify
> *I bear witness with blood dripping from the moss with*
> *ropes grappling my branches and the singe of fire*
> *around my trunk. I stand here to be a witness.*

Out of the deep fissures of the Great Oak's bark the names will pour,
slow and heavy, the weight of evidence will be pulled from the Oak's
   roots.
> *the sap will speak, we bear evidence, oh Lawd*
> *of this man's inhumanity.*

The roots will reach down yonder to those 805 steel columns in Montgomery,
Alabama,
where more evidence has been memorialized. The known and unknown names
will rise up to speak of the inhumanity of this man.

And God will waive his right hand, and the wind will be great, and the trees
will be asked to speak, the Great Oaks will rise, will not cry, but they will
scream.

*Leon Forrest book title edited by Toni Morrison

Emmett Till's Reinter

Carolyn Brant's lie.

The shadow box   concealed
      under plank floorboards
buried beneath filth's hell lays—
  her lies.

As if the box's shell— were a white chalk shadow,
a shroud, a cover-up of withered   concealed
  rectitude   crammed inside.

Fog-crusted glass   its contents   if she dares
to break the seal   a vaporous stench
        dead flesh
        dried blood on rusted metal.

Fingerprints of the secrets   that buried a—life.
The shadow box   the truth in her hands,
      again   tossed
into the Tallahatchie River.

How Many Ways to Say Boy

He smiles, laughs, and says
>*my dad knows your dad, Joe Willie*

Joe   Willie?

Joe Willie?
It's my eyes that demand truth from this white man
Who continues to smile and speaks
>*yeah my dad would see your Dad all the time at the airport*

My Dad at the airport
Yes, my Dad works as a Skycap, TWA, then US Air
his 2nd job, he takes care of his family, so we take summer vacations
to distant places.

This white man with forked smiles says
>*my dad said that Joe Willie was the best basketball player on*
>*the Aliquippa team when they were in school.*

Truth, my dad always said he was the best, but then the best then
did not get him a scholarship to a university, not then, not there,
but it got him to the steel mill, to the most dangerous place this
side of hell.

My eyes glare at this white man in a white shirt, dark tie, leaning
back in his chair, smiling as though he is visioning himself making
those baskets.

He has yet to answer the question rolling around in my head
smashing against my temples
>*Who is this Joe   Willie?*

I'm not trippin' I know my own Daddy's name

Whoa, a short reprieve, for this white man, in the white shirt, who
dreams of shooting baskets as good as my Dad—
   hold your horses my Dad's youngest brother's name is Willie
   perhaps, um, no he was too young to be playing, well may
   be then my mind like the whipping branch chastises me

and the name slowly enters my mouth, first it tries me, to jump down
my throat. I hold it in my mouth, and it begins to fight for its life, and
I chew the words and spit them out.

I could still sense the nasty taste in my mouth when visiting my Dad that Sunday

He was big on family dinners.
We found ourselves bounded
to each other around the dinner
table.

I said, Daddy
   this white guy whose dad went to school with you kept calling you
   Joe Willie
I knew what he was going to say before he said it,
but I needed his confirmation, as folks have mentioned
at times that I be trippin.

My Daddy's smile eclipsed, like memories of balled fists

Another way of calling us boy
   was to add Willie to your name

   his dad was one of the many racists we had to deal with
   growing up.

   Time changes, names change, but racism sounds the same—
   boy, nigger, willie. They always wanted to make sure you
   knew they believed they were better than you.

My Daddy's name is Joseph Lewis Lee.

Shhh!

my daddy robbed a bank
a long time ago

shhhhhhhhh
I was teased   **once**   by a classmate
in grade school

no many how many times mrs.
bowers tattled to my parents at PTO
night, that she caught me chewing
gum in class, my mom would come
home angry with me, did she know the
next time I chewed gum, mrs. bowers
stood over me, and gave me an entire pack
of fruit stripped gum, five strips, to chew at
once, then ordered me to put that glob of gum
on the tip of my nose till the end of class?
no one teased me about that gum sitting
on my nose

shhhh
and my parents made sure I had money
to buy lots and lots of scholastic books
no one in class could out read me

shhhh
they bought me gray hush-puppy tie-up shoes
to wear on those highly polished wood floors
of Sewickley Grade School
where I could not wait to be in the 6th grade to
sing the little drummer boy song at the christmas
concert

shhhhh
walking home from school
him and his cousin would every day
run behind us, calling us skinny legs and
pulling up our dresses and laughing
but when my daddy

shhhhhhh
robbed that bank
he teased me
the only one who teased me

about
my daddy robbing a bank

he said something like yea
your daddy's in jail for robbing a bank

I kept
silent
cause if I was as mean as I am now
I would have spat *your daddy ain't*
neva been around, so how we know
you even got a daddy?

yep, but I was not mean yet, so I just
looked at him and so did everyone else
I remember my best friend Dee-Dee
was there, some older boys were nearby,
but after that day he never teased me again
about

my daddy robbing a bank
shhh.

Midnight Shift
> *Black Steelworkers at J&L*

North, juke joints, frenzy feet tapped
tore-up floors to city fingerpicked guitars
quicker than field boys' jigs, flying dice
against back cement walls.

> *We're gonna jump down turn around*
> *pick a bale of cotton*
> *jump down turn around pick a bale a day.*

Daddy's bandana survived drenched sweat of crop
fields, now nicked fire hurled from liquefied orange
steel, spiritual hymn of steel mills, heaven, hot,
hades. No cool creek by the field, no cool rains.

Foundation of soot and iron shaves plasters
skin. His croaky lungs sounds like bullfrogs long
ways off, Alabama ponds, hushed shadows.
Jump up Friday nights, boogie on threadbare
linoleum floors, with loose women and drink.

> *Me and my gal can pick a bale of cotton,*
> *Me and my gal can pick a bale a day.*

Brothers, uncles, came, 1950s, crammed tight
Oil-stench squares, burst in spurts at Pittsburgh
station. Scattered folks, northern towns, sideroads,
brown shanties built along Ohio, muddy rivers,
dirt roads of Aliquippa, Homestead, Braddock.

Mother, children, abandoned wood shotgun houses,
wax paper windowpanes where sun crept through
one room, where lovemaking, Bible reading shared
quarters. Kettles cradled okra, collards, hominy.

Wind-carried aroma deposited on line-dried clothes,
stomped by creek rocks, whop, whop, whoop. Cotton
-bred backs courted steel mills. Provider, protector,
or slicksters who walk with a dip .

     Jump down, turn around

Chains of men, raw callused hands, flung 100-pound
cotton bags over shoulders; strong tendons pulled
thighs and shoulders tight, blistered fingers
buried under rough leather gloves, grip, lift,
greet glowing ingots, tossed like cotton bales.

     Lordy, pick a bale of cotton

Daddy told all those we left behind, we's gonna be rich.
                                      *Leadbelly *Pick a Bale of Cotton*

Disturbance of Placement
> *to sit with Gwendolyn Brooks & Derrick Bell*

foreign immigrants, stolen visitors in this
land, of our fathers. our faith lays in things
not seen, neither felt, nor tasted. it is a learnt
experience, to be an undesirable—
    in familiar places.
> *—once upon a time*
> *people possessed*
> *ancient healings—*

places of things buried in coastal sands. in
red clay foundations of memories. caught in
gracious nets. sagas wrapped in orange cocoons
of indigo. of weaved tree barks that bend tides
of winds. narratives tucked in sweetgrass
baskets. thick sentiments, nutrients transferred
from roots of cotton's soft curls.
> *—it's sunday eve,*
> *girls with shiny hair,*
> *scent of bergamot, sit*
> *on kitchen stools and*
> *hold both ears—*

someone knows our names. names seized when
the bough broke and names plummeted to the
ground; drowned in rivers. names trapped, burned
> *—a telephone call,*
> *a gunshot, drags*
> *you from the bed,*
> *a late-night knock,*
> *death is at the door.—*

in the quiet spots, paths of blood's spittle left tracks
from where we came. not towards this bizarre place,
but to a place, named our own. our sanctuary. place
where foot meets earth, palms to drums, sounds leap
and fly to far-off, sacred places. Far from this alien land,
this dead space, this place of metal shrapnel that cuts our
skin, this place of subterranean voices.
   —when did we stop
   breathing the sweet
   ocean's air—

Dreams of Drowning in the Ocean's Sky

fear of the

ocean

not afraid, we

will

drown, but heavy

with

anxiety,

that

we will, adapt

and

travel the

ocean

floors filled with

micro

-cells of

ancestors,

    —will be the air

    we breathe as

    we settle on

    the ocean's

    floor—

who we were taught

did not

survive, but

drowned with

bones scattered,

on the

ocean's floor

from the

coast of Africa

to

the dampness of

low

-land islands,

a fruitage

of angel, and

blue

bottle trees.

Grandma Weaves Sweetgrass in Her Plaits

Indigo-stained fingers
worn like a leather coat
handed down from mother
to daughter to daughter
to daughter, then handed
back to the mother of
daughters as she sits in
the wood slat chair
with short peg legs that
sink deep in the moist earth.
she points her long curved
finger towards the angel
tree and closes her eyes,
and a simple whisper of a
prayer leaves her lips.
small and thin they part
almost unnoticeably, but
the prayers slip   from
her lips, to the ears of
the angel oak tree . at that
moment the wind whistles
through the tree that blooms
cobalt bottles, a trap for bad
dreams, for those haints who
chase you in dreams. her
indigo-stained fingers tenderly
trace   the glass. fingers that
have held the evil in her
family's dreams and released
in the morning. her stained
fingers, held in a prayer
stance wipe   her tears
and she breathes in.

In the Wake of Gospel #1 … and in the Beginning

[repeated low pitch of a tambourine]

She grew up with the Holy Ghost, with the
spirit cloaking on folks. Feet, arms filching,
with shout circles and tongues- speaking.

Up and down church aisles, members race.
No one trips on frayed rugs, or purses, or
babies, or other spirit-stricken Sunday-go-
to-meeting bodies laid out in the aisles,
laid out in the pews.

Old ladies snap out, with big hats intact,
with their arms up, arms down, crying like
40 days and nights during that one song with
five encores, that have members leaping up
in praise.

Those rattles take hold of their feet, gospel
filled with tambourines' tin-tin-na-bulation
and drums. The revival tent explodes as the
shouts to glory cut through the August
night's inferno wind melts the tar and stone
streets of Aliquippa's Plan 11. That
burnt light in the night, bright as J&L's steel
mill flames thrown up from hades.

The tent, a beacon of lights and sweat from
down the hill, pitched on a field of marmalade
dirt, that hallowed-be-thy-name place. It all
feels so ancestral, like it came on a hurricane
through the middle passage, to catch you up,
to remind you where you came.

[repeated mid pitch of a tambourine]

The music draws, in the shouts, the hand claps,
the choir's sway, to the piano's beat, in sync
feet rally with the drum's beat, voices holler
for Moses to come on down.

She senses the voices inside her, come alive,
they call to her, like the ancestors, they can
not be silenced nor forgotten, they lie under
neath the cross, sealed in the tomb, under
neath music and scriptures, the tongues speak.

Unfamiliar language jumps up from folks
whose tongues are stolen Sundays by the
Holy Ghost, DNA's prophecy.

[mummers of *thank you Jesus, thank you, Jesus]*

It all comes out as they speak in tongues, in
a language un-spoken. A language of tongues
from inside, inside deep, a language that jumps
out of mothers and the choir as their hands
perform that fast double then triple handclap,
that, that, sanctified clap when palms of your
hands sweat, and sting, and you cannot stop
when the Holy Ghost snatches you.

In the middle of a shout—when HG grabs
hold of your spirit, you lose control— all you
are able to do is scream *Jesus, ah mahmah.*

When all you do is jump and wrap your arms
around your body and then tears come a-rolling,
and like a wave of virus, one by one members'
arms fly up, they hold themselves and turn
around, turn around, and turn around, in the
midnight hour, they say He turns it around,
and here you are, Sunday, and you cannot speak,

but your arms make gestures in the air, because
language was not always spoken, but it was
first written in the air.

[repeated high pitch of a tambourine]

The church mothers wave their white lap-napkins
as members race around the church. They run fast
like they chasing that good thang, and the folks
in the pews mumble thank you, Jesus. All those
thanks, and the sweat underneath the wigs comes
down hard like Moses all pissed from the mountain
when he saw the people acting all crazy and
disrespectful.

The sweat comes down on the church, and the music
the gatekeeper of the frenzy, is full of the Holy Ghost,
as the church breaks out in the Holy Ghost
sanctified dance, and members leap out of
seats, doing whatever they did last night at
the club, cause it is all happy dances, says the
DNA in that Pentecostal clap, and the church is
Rocking, and it is loud with the sounds of the
"talking in tongues." And everyone jumps up,
and fans fan, but the heat is thick, and folks
swim in their own sweat, the runners still in
their race to glory. This is church, this is
revival.

[repeated low pitch of a tambourine]

And that is when she first sensed there were tongues
inside her, stirring up her insides, birthing their
way through the canals of languages, through
hand claps, tears, and Holy dances, and she knew
one day the tongues would speak out of her.

In the Wake of Gospel—Space in the Hull

The taste of tears as it slips from your lips to your tongue as you moan
  in praise.
—Gospel songs hold space.

How we navigate these spaces of the unknown of the familiar when
tongues twist.
In this space are ocean waves of voices found in this holding space.

Palms meet, and the sweat feels like mud clay, smells like delta silt, smells
like hulls of ships, smells like blood that flows from women.
—Blood holds this space.

The waves that hit the hull sound like beats of hardened feet, sound
like gatherer hands,
—Sounds holds this space.

An empty deafening sound carried from the coasts of Africa to the jagged
coast of this strange place.

In the quietness, the waves hit low, sound like women chanting, palms
hitting shields.
—Sounds hold the distance of space.

And left is the wave wake that followed those in the hulls to the edges of
  what
—sounds like death.

Be still in this space, tongues cry, and speak.
—Speaking tongues hold this space.

Prayer

after reading Zora Neale Hurston

ah seen tha brown 'n black rattler crawlin' rund
dem blackberry bushes.

em sweet smells gat hold a tha snake, but he kept
sneakin back tryin to bit em berries

black a full of juice. ole rattler got greedy, snatched
berries and barbs, choked,

dat ole snake like dat ms ruby red polish she wor
on her nails.

mah christian-amen grandma said, *"red ez devil's
juice, choke ya, lak dat ole snake."*

ms ruby's juice gat hol of my pappy, ev'ry sat'day
nite.

grandma prayed fuh mah ma, "gawd, mak her strong
fuh sun'day mornin."

an ah prayed fah rattler tuh bit ms ruby dead.

A Prayer Learnt from Her Pentecostal Mother

A religious fanatic, she is not.
She believes in the
       Father, Son, Holy Ghost,
also
       vampires, aliens, and ghosts.

Her sensitivity an open door, a tormented soul,
       an invite to: restless dead, a sporadic inter-
       ruption of sweet dreams.

Her first, a shadow, a woman, who sat crossed-legged
balanced on the edge of her white princess dresser.
They slither like sinister villains who burst through
midnight's veil.

Her night routine: her toes ram weathered natural cotton,
a torn piece of clothing, basic dark shades across the bottom
of her bedroom door. Closing off open space small enough
for the Wazimamoto to slink through. A lesson of survival
handed down from her ancestor Vodou Queen *Marie Laveau—*
with each cram she repeats,
       "the blood of Jesus, the blood of Jesus."

Rosary Prayers

Dyin ain't pretty. Sure ain't streets dyin. Pretty ain't it. In multi-plex
castles, Black women die, wrinkled, prayin for enemies, rockin dead
weight. Praisin hard life. Lives lonely, lives. Many teared eyes, full
drops. Rough hands ain't neva been pretty. Ironin. Washin. Cookin.
Spread table, legs, okra, hominy, mush. Vines, faces twisted. Eyes
redd up. Woulda. Coulda. If lovin a Black man is a full stomach:
malnutrition stalks Black women. If basics, held jobs. Mothers, so
many, on knees. Arched hearts. Spines bent, heavy vessels. Laid down.
Love no more. Love unknown songs of mothers. Restricted to marches.
For mothered sons. Not plenty lovin. Black women lovin canned tight.
Untouched on sale shelves. Hardened, faded. Run-away lovin. Caught
in snared lives. Chalk bags stuffed. Muffled screams. Knuckled heads,
fists, faced palms out. A wasted submission. Lovin dyin ain't pretty.
Black women's hearts-

I C U

Sedates choirs.

exposure of swaggeritis, our bodies are housed in ICU, break tongues,
roll air- dismantled throat, legs, bones, coiled hairs, crunched, stretched
with metal rollers, lye to the side, in efforts to tame matted manes—face
mask pricks cheek bones, lips, butt, curious to surgical transformation.
Features chiseled—no, they do not desire us, similar to—they want us
to—disappear—to be, to come to be, small in stature—mouthpiece,
breathe drunken, air restricted; inhale fairy dust, nothing left to believe
—from within—hijacked air, air hijacked, repulse, slow pulse, abandoned,
exiled, exhaled—we are from the inside dying, clouded signals sucked
into their own eruption, not as clear nor as skies fair as predicated [MLK]
—or are we lost, or found eden's desolated parade as "we made it," yet we
still placebos—victims of our own transparency—we fake second sight,
we blind as monkeys chase music, chase non-cents—our existence
ceases resistances; we resist to exist. Sit here chillin—gonna smoke
these blunts and chill some more.

Voices silent.

Even the Ratchet Pray

He must have had time: downtime, between folks tearing up his hem, stealing his fingerprints, those desperate & drunk in faith, cattlecall   for a healing, or two. Mass protest to save the children, now new-jack—save cats & dogs too. Pimped-out streaming prophets' infomercials- any given Sunday while worldly emptiness shakes barren pockets for coins, in attempts to purchase healings—20% off sale [expires after midnight strokes] to ward off risky contagious sickness. Shadows cast in shades of roses hot for His touch and sleight of hand to reclaim sight. A packaged healing—mix with faith, juice, or Pink Catawba to rise up real sham. While the worldly & swine sit back, chillax, glass in hand & laugh, because it feels good, feels good to laugh. Feels good grass underfoot & between thin sheets. The world laughs at its atrocities, indecently blameless. But in its dark corners of the "hush-hush," "don't tell," one by one, they tumble & fall to their knees. Did Jesus? Laugh, ever?

**"Fire & Lies" #88hundred25thousand2 Ways to Say America
  Is Not Beautiful**

even within your silence, we still hear the crackle of flames
and smell the scent of kerosene thrown heavy-handed against
crossings of knotted wood sinking in the damp dirt of darkness.

Disturb the sound of silence

It   speaks
          in rips
          in tugs
          in sharp
pangs

There are no limitations
          no oppressed
arena, where it canNot
          be
          spoken

Loud interruptions
          call the ushers—
it is a movie
          dammit

Palestine lessons root
bridges built of
          lead
flying spiders web
          latched land mines
lands   common grounds
embed seedlings in urban fields
playground where flowers
stoned
          buried still
alive

its language flip-cops
          holes
sinks in quicksand pools
hidden graves of
          prettiness

gaping mouth sings
songs   obstructs snaps
        chokes

gingerly spanks through pillows
        or   windows
Your uncle speaks it
        fluently
if not him, a brother/cousin
        a gone Boo gone
Who bled out cause his dialect
was slurred
        patent leather blood
smears on hardened red clay
        Bricks and stones will
hurt bones but
        break for noise
laughs
        and cums on itself
it is feeling
        its-self
it is language   sunder's
        Grammy
Award music

front row smug smiles smug
Ocars sits piled on concrete
        platforms
listens its sweetness pings off
        walls
shrapnel vowels sharp
        brush
stabs
paint portraits of new dumb
        tied tongue

against
        back teeth makes
less sound
submissive fallen forts
        X missing
chromosomes

Sounds to arm-aments
        rebellious but which
fight   which right
        side
which cement fence
        peppered peepholes
spy out
        or hails jail
its twin barrels boogey
get down to its captive lulls
        sleep tight hypocrites
sing chorus
        Pings rapidly
unbalance each night
hide it
        hide it
dive
underneath
        its voice
prints vapors.

No One Ever
chile, go get grandma her matches from the kitchen drawer

the popping sound on the mic
the flick the spark when mothers
speak   after
being asked about their Black child
after an unanswered injustice has been
committed
against their Black child

when silence is—frag-mented
when the scent of sulfur fills the mic

no one ever:
muthafucka i will burn you and this
muthafuckin city down. you better arrest,
charge with murder, and put on trial who
did this to my child, who hurt my child in
this way, my child is dead
        and grandma needs her matches

my baby is dead because they dared to talk,
to reach—for a driver's license / asked why?
said they have rights

no one ever:
i swear I am going to burn down this city
your house with your entire family
then take your ashes and dunk
them in gasoline and light ya ass up
again

who did this to my child? who killed
my child?

the streets filled with silence
continue sounds of turning cheeks
echoes in   silence

No one ever:
do you hear me? do you hear me?
muthafucka?
do you fuckin hear me?

They Have Been Warned Repeatedly, with No Effect

tell me

what is going on   over [t]here

beneath the mind of folks
blues folks
po folks

don't you know
don't you
you don't you know

the air is thick with past tenses
still what's going on

tell me
tell me

what language you speaking
in those poems   in those blues   notes

wails overriding the world's wind turbines
tell me
tell me
tell me

do i have to beg
brothers   i will   beg

if you tell me what's going on
what's hidden in the minds of
po folks
blues folks

come on brothers
tell me tell me

air is thick as karo syrup

hot as tulsa's flames all-
consuming yet   we walk
out the   flames

sister sisters tell me
what's happening
what you

you know you hanging out
those windows of Mecca while
ashes catch fire to your coils,
burn your cheeks flushed

black red glows of ash gather on your
sill
sisters   sister girl tell me
what we gonna do

about this fire in the air
what we gonna do

the fire moving lazy
it has a universe of time to burn
been burning

been burning   generations
burning fields
burning bodies that hanged

like flames bodies jump
bodies do the jerk as they turn into
flames   burning cross this
country   fire dances cross water

taut fire lines burst between countries
between people who dare you dare you
to cross the line

what's going on
tell
me
what   we gonna do.

bout the fire that jumps
from here to there

places occupied with hate

burn we gonna burn it down

what we gonna
do
poet folks
blues folks

what we gonna do
tell me.

what we gonna do
sisters brothers
about this fire in the air.

Morpheus Whispering

if a Black body falls
to the ground
does it make a sound

when—a Black body hits
concrete does it
make a wave

does its breath
hold on
till the last exhale
is not enough to
meet an
inhale

does the body
fall
like a confederate statue

or drop
like a green trash bag
filled with earthly belongings

does the body
when it hits or drops to
the ground
          bounce

does the entire body
die at one time

or do the legs tremble
and create an intimate
ceremonial dance &
leave their torso behind

the arms, do they lurch up or
forward in an attempt to hold
on to life

when a body twitches
does that mean it hears the
              music

what kind of sound would a
Black body that falls to the
ground, that hits the concrete
make

could it sound bold and bright
an offshoot of miles davis's lips
meeting its mouthpiece

—Black bodies do not die
but metamorphosis into tunes
played out loud in splashes
of libation liquor.

Milk Overcoats Being Worn in Ferguson

1.
Unshackle yourself from
SONnets, cute couplets, get from
under the degrees, publishable
assimilated prose.

Take back the night truths
as your lines unCOVER the lies
of violence against your brothers,
take that plausible leap back
into the BAM of it all, back into
REAL time and TURN UP the
saturation TURN UP the volume
TURN UP the world, Poets
as ya'll supposed to do.

2.
Don't let gas cover, the wooden
bullets bury truth, told by spies
who lie and want us to all DIE.

MOURNing to America
this BEAutiful day after night
of peaceful thoughts turned
why not modern-day genocide
they all fucking animals.

It burns the thing inside it. And that thing screams
after Amiri Baraka

We
Are
those
whose
bodies
are
shields.

Whose bodies
are
documentation.

Whose bodies are shields
able to
bend metal
bars.

Whose bodies are shields
able to
deflect bullets
silver and the gold
lead and the buckshot.

We
Are
those
who fly
above clouds
hurricanes and bullshit.

We
Are
those
who practice
respectfully
cleanse
our bodies
with petals
earth mother's
flesh
earth mother's
blood.

Purification
in oranges, in bright
pinks, in yellows
and green breaths
and releases
silent sound waves
always the
drums
always the
drums.

Tongues
language of
Sankofa
beneath the belly
back of throat

to tip of tongues
yaaalaaaa
yaaalaaaa
yaaalaaaa.

We
Are
those ears
always hearing
drums.

We
Are those feet
pulled up from
ground, walks
on air, climb
plateaus
mountaintops
treetops.

We
those whose bodies
ride
waves like
roller skates
like walking
skipping on
water
we live

here
not knowing
how great we
are spiritually.

What our ancestors
planted in
us.

We are our ancestors'
creations.

We are who our ancestors
said
WeareWeare
WeareWeare
WeareWeare
WeareWeare

We
Are.

Blame It on the Wooden Arks, Blame It on Those Boogeymen

Believe
      y'all   believe
What they think (truth)
to make us think (their truth) is truth

      Lies, fabricated tales, stolen
          as they were told   revealed

"No more auction block for me., No more, no more"

First thou three, those three wooden arks, anti-sanctified sails
      filled with pillaged-grimms took first-class middle passage,
      crossed the Atlantic sea, de-flowered ships.

Wooden arks filled with "crimes-to-be-announced"
      start with the Pequot, it was massacre, masked in thanks

Boogeymen in the shade of light crashed on that rock
      busting up on folks stealing and stuff, you know
      how thieves do . . .

Call it what you want, history no longer shackled to his-story tales
      told sea to shining sea.

I'm no traitor, a realist though, the bones tell the tale
      buried coast-to-coast long as riverbeds
Before they came life flowed,
      AleutInuitChinookChumashApacheComancheCrowSioux
      IroquoisMassachusetCreekPomoNezPerceShoshonePueblo

Into Disney flamboyance rewrites
        Jiving Crows, Sunflower [Centaur's pickaninny slave], Peter's Indians
        Uncle Remus, Aladdin, Princess and the Frog, Tonto, Pocahontas
Excuse while I bust out in song
        Zip-a-dee-doo-dah, zip-a-dee-ay
Wooden arks gang planks, freed thieves, lynchmen dare I say
terrorists   yes   thank you   fondling fathers

Old Ben lifted too   (what you get for teaching **them your** language),
        chunks of words from Iroquois Great Law of Peace
        hid them in the constituted US Da truth.

Thievery.

Wait for It—It Is the New World Genocidal Crow

Share folks, Instagram party vines, drunk cats, hotmess dj'ing ghetto
mix, selfish selfies, folks giving, not not-free breakfast lines. Pokes,
likes, bomb social hoods, drones bomb Gaza; drones get closer to
us/US via Amazon. Me-occupied games, fingers grope screens. Hand
games, clap slap, clap slap.

meanwhile monkey got choked, New, New, York. There is enough to
spray around. Canisters bodysurf crowds jeer. It's not over. On? It is
going . . . Share it. Free fall Ferguson. Blackflip out of sight (out
of mind). Long time dead bodies, ignite. Black-out, media led
regression. Palms up, clap slap

palms up down. Freed of gun (can of soda), gun (Skittles), gun
(driver's license). Uphold, hold up. Hot, Black skin. Not cause it
pops on stage. Grinds in clubs. Too cool, Gwen said. Foolish fools.
Now melanin needs gun-screen. Get ready. Here it comes. It's gots
to come—human rights. Military turnt up. When they

tattoo yo ass. Messy lives if a way not found, stop this madness, stop
crowd feet's pound, thousands deep. Candles/stuffed bears—not again.
It is gonna be Soweto, gonna be—Red Cliff Indian killing grounds,
gonna be—segregation & gentrification's mulatto children. Every side-
walk crack a Black foot, step in

the name of Ferguson, New York, Pittsburgh, Oakland. Delivers blows
via new legal poachers—police, givers of excessive trickery, it's going
on, it's going . . .

We Are Accountable

after Tamara J Madison's "Till Poem"

but you see i am the angel—of death
a vengeful angel
the angel on the other side of your coin

with these wings of death i sing
songs of vengeance

sounds in octaves of a high C pitch—can
you—even hear me coming
as i travel from city to towns
with mud crusted feet through backwater places
to countries surrounded by water, or
mountains surrounded by forest

those places where you shine in the middle
of gaslights, in swamp-covered roads, dusty
narrow paths, paved highways marred by tollbooths
we have to pay one way

I walk on earth, not touching the ground
or brick sidewalks
or tar-covered backstreets
where you feel you are invisible
where you are invincible

not so easy, to hide from my lover—
he dresses in a black suit, cut just so
to show off his ab-bility to take you on—he is
a winner

i continue to move down these streets
fearless as death has already visited
i am death's sidepiece, moving
sharply among the living as a reminder
of death, to remember the scent of
bloodletting ceremonies, the stink of
genocide, of self-hate
yes, we are all accountable for the blood

in humble feet i travel all places
where black bodies, brown bodies
are scarified
are laid side by side
feet to feet
reflection of the hulls of death
chained by bullets

my wings are heavy
there is strength in my backbone
my shoulders bear the burden of
death
won't you come fly with me

Death Doula's Song

> *Dying has become foreign to us and it's having some devastating effects. Because we don't know what death looks like, what it sounds like, what it feels like, it has given rise to a lot of fear and anxiety.*

—Mariam Ardati, death doula

death, we know is an unknown but confirmed destiny, but if i could, let me be ready. i would want my going home met with joy, with goodbye to this life, and hello to home, with drums, with songs, with doulas that bring life into this world with warmth and guide you out with as much warmth. light scented candles, fill the room with flowers and plants that emit fresh air. fill the room with hums, with music from the desert, from the forest, from the mountains, from the jungles, from the west to the north, to the east, to the southern hemispheres. from the concrete streets, from the green grassy plateaus. let the thunder and lightning sing the chorus of my earthly life, let the moon and sun carry me home. rub my body with my favorite scented oils, massage my face, my arms, my legs, my neck, this ritual. loudly speak lines from my favorite poems. speak loudly lines of my poems that were my favorites. word spoken out of mouths of family, friends, to soothe my soul. speak of this better place, a place of no pain, a place of peace, a safe place. a place where happiness jumps excitedly, to greet me. a place where my language is that of all my ancestors; finally, a place where I understand the songs coming off the waves of the atlantic whisper to me what will be found in this paradise. the treasure that will be mine. you need to know, so you too, will be happy. face me towards the sun. i was born under the sun. let my wrapped body find home in the sun's warmth. allow the sins of my life to disintegrate out an opened window as the sage burns, my last smells be of my mother's freshly baked cinnamon buns. this is not a death trip but a pilgrimage to the promised land. that place I was promised. send me in my death wrap of silks and soft cotton dyed in shades of purple, orange, yellow, and indigo, wrap me from head to toe, with cotton tassel ties at the head, waist, and feet. let the hums of the end-of-life doula weave with yours. sing me to that beautiful place.

Nina's Fire: Frantic's Go-Go

For we're creatures of the wind and
wild is the wind

        —Nina Simone

Storm's thunder flush Nina's heart.
Tempest's path of chaotic currents,
Travel time, in one's own mind
     Voudou zombie's taunts, *it's real, it's real.*
Punishments: metronome's off   beats
Barbed wired blues, blacks' vibrations
Burst against freedom's white   spaces.
    Goddam

       Goddam
No joke—its mind fed mannerisms, clenches
Down on ya thoughts   oppressive airways
Unhinges manic movements   deadly tango
Rhythm, nomadic & grounded & no madness
Blue's bi-moods: Damballa's dance & stalk
    Knows

       Knows everybody
Wrestles for space: facets of Nina's soul
Partner with some lone, no   one
Each one, everyone's lynched   breath.
Detonates, showers, hammers   fiction.
    Can't you see

       Can't you see it
Reading bones   thrash milky's brilliant ways
Crossroads between Nina's honest debates &
Last calls. Her woman-led fortified songs, hoards
Days after tomorrow & tomorrow's days after.
    I don't belong

       I don't belong here
Heaps yesterday's wingless fleas
Stuck to summer's window screens
Screams   look out, out there, seekers
Hiders, come in, come on in, olly, olly
Oxen free: Nina's pleads—*Goddam*
       Goddam.

When the Walls Close In

when women were the ones to
dress the dead
the dead drugged out from rivers
the dead littered in street gutters
uncovered for hours until the yellow tape
withered

bodies dead, disrespected, that disgusting
taste left in mouths
that sets up house in their minds

countless screams, and they cry
and they cry
and they cry
cry
and they
cry

and they walk from one wall to next
with their tight fists
and they walk from the window to
the wall
and people sit outside their doors
and they cry
and they curse, cause
they cry, and
they don't know what else to do

the trauma confesses itself in their minds
a trigger reaction to the release of the
triggers
the clicks on repeat
like the moon disappears in the day
but it is—but it is still there

the trauma reflects in windows
and mirrors, and words
found written on yellow wallpaper

In Our Room by Ourselves

we cry. monsoons erode our bodies.
like earthquakes of mudslides
this physical nothingness trembles to
wails echoing cross continents and oceans.
the gravel beneath our bare feet tremor.

the ground opens—a sinkhole. a flush of
soil and we, disappear. we are buried with
mouths exposed. a waxen lid, the earth
entombs our bodies. our tears flood rivers.
seal our eyes. light is not required to see

paths of stars, electric dream patterns. and,
we sleep as the earth constrains our bodies.
the pressure snaps bones, tendons spring
free. our skin explodes and we, are hurled
in every direction. we are compost,

flung across the universe. our veins stretch
the longitudes and latitudes of victories.
yet,we bleed. from our eyes. our noses. our ears.
soles of our feet. palms of our hands. we bleed
out from our brains. our mouths stitched shut.

our vaginas preserved as pickled yams. yet we
sing. what space, inside our room, rejoices in
chants? we are the earth's core. buried and torn
apart, thrown as treasure in a scavenger hunt,
to be found. we wait. to be found. and we wait.

Public Notice: Women Next

They—will, come for us, after streets are cleaned of chalked frames; exploited skin
dries in midday sun, burns through asphalt, smells of rubber, and fresh Poke,
waits to die on tongues that whisper 'round corners netting—speaks *"they coming"*

us multi-hued bangles, polychrome textile fabric skirts and hips bang, splash
paint on crowded living rooms, food plastered on yesterday's meals, menu of stolen
this and thats, coupons for empty houses stamped, and bare refrigerators, sticky

patched linoleum, that ever after, returns to that place, of suffice rage, drank like
red kool aide in bandaged bottles, shrouded in pulp wrapped twisted twine, that
refuses to endure change—

"for us"—mascu-packs Delhi buses hustle dusty roads lined by India's strange
trees—bloom feministic scent, splittail petals hums Sangeet, "they coming for us."

Restless myths hack fertility, as inverted hymens polish machetes. Congo drums
hypnotize herded girls, whose hems unravel in butchery's blood, beaded bangles
bounce off drums, diminishes Mandela's freedom walk, peace buried in collapsed
minds—*"they coming, for us"*— now.

Jesup, Georgia, in the Dark

This place sweats of paper and rotted coffee grounds
as dust ejects off backs of rusted, open truck beds.

Young woman with skin that almost matches the darkening
sky stands under the planked roof of a makeshift BBQ joint
that seems only open during football Friday nights when
coloreds come in town.

Or on two weekdays, but not this day, when it doubles as the
counter for Greyhound business.

Other days passengers stand roadside under its puckered roof
for protection [weather related only].

Young woman stands in prayer for alternative protection. Her hands
sweat in the chill of the night. She clutches hold of the handle of
her rolling suitcase as though it's a tearaway weapon. Then wonders
why knives, tear gas, or guns are not allowed to be packed in luggage
when waiting in the darkness, alone in a southern swamp town's back
street, in front of deserted storefront, situated in the middle of an empty
pitch-black endless highway, which seems to only go south.

Places where ghosts drift in and watch her as she waits.

Places where a young woman alone not knowing how far the
wayward Greyhound has to lug upwards from Jacksonville, Florida, to
Jesup, Georgia.

Her eyes eagle sight, watch as they circle the block.
Young white boys ride five-deep in an opened jeep with
wheels armored in back road mud. With mouths wide and
hawkeyed on the hunt target her each time they drive-by.

MISSISSIPPI

bloated bodies   those floaters
      mississippi's   mud pies.

pallbearers' footprints   blood baptized
after the neck snaps
after the bough breaks
after the nigger chase   is won.

bodies hidden under floorboards
underground, in root cellars.
      who will sing for bodies found in the river?

mothers want to know—if bodies be drunk with
bullets—if a leg be missing—if the penis be shoved
in mouths—

cause it is, the black women who clean the bodies
try to make them honorable for burial.

twine tight round necks
stomachs slashed opened   filled with river rocks
and the river   rocks
      take me to the river   *take me to the river*
      take me to—

the dragged bodies—are—yanked to river's edge, found by
the light of the silver moon—shine   had   nothing to do
with the howls heard,

howls pour out of darkness
      a shot glass filled with dark liquor
      guzzled down, burns   fleshy throats.

the flesh filled with bullets, the hog-tied flesh
flesh dragged up, from the river's gut.

Sweet Land of Alabaster Cities

this twisted skin / that seeps in its venom like / slime left at a snail's
pace on side of walks / on wet leaves / that fall / that fall.

the skin on the ground / this skin scalped from muscles / laid out like
hulled animals / with their horns and hooves and teeth / in sealed boxes.

with bones—suckling sticks to strangers.

this skin left exposed / to address the alienated-nation / a cross-dresser's
host of flesh and blood-let.

let blood / swallowed slowly from / tiny marrows of the decayed.

Take My Bloodletting

"take me to the water, take me to the water"

to places where
we sing
to places where we plant
a harvest of peace

take my skin
wear it to the places where
we are free
where the soil is cool
and the earth is at rest

heal

take this poem
chant this poem
create songs
rebuild

walk this path paved
with our history of protest
of sweet resistance
and ripe with love

heal

let our laughter
let our tears
let our pain

let the music of the ocean
the clap of thunder
the whirl of tornadoes
and bow down to our knees

heal

take life's harmony
the sounds of melodies
from a place where
we are free
and safe

take the images of the cross
of raised hands
of praisesongs
sung in languages a thousand fold

and let the deaths
of many
so many
of so many

the deaths
of so many
take the prayers
take the hollowness
of our fires

and heal

Take Us to the Water

go to the water's edge and let it all out

scream till you have no voice

until you find your voice

go to the water
you will not drown

let your arms wave in the air like a flag
you long to hold of colors that reflect
your face as it embraces the ocean

not that stifled scream that has you
on your knees at night

scream, like freedom kisses

scream, like you found
what you did not know
what you were in search of

scream like the search
found you

scream like the water
is warm and you are
bound to the womb again

scream like you are safe

take to the water's edge
and jump

Courageous Acts of Being

belts   of ocean slap   against rocks   then
rolls gently to fill empty spaces

if living breaths of Black women's skin, were
sounds of implosions from   in in inside

& hummingbirds in veiled   trees
peck peck pecker-wood pecks

if being Black skin were   sounds
of destruction

crows black and brilliant and blaring
fly and nest on live wires, waits to
let shit—drop

if Black women's skin were sounds
crackling pig skin, burnt scraps drown
in the bottom of the caste-iron of used
oil

half-drunk gin bottles flung against table's edge
flesh ripped, spurts of blood pelts the floor
if dying Black skin were sounds, and

skin so silent it whimpers, and its claws were
hurricanes (katrina, her sisters, and em) shatter
the hate of the earth's crust, hate that cries loud
and hard to silent Black women's breaths

if the breath of Black women were   sounds, were
rumbles, were thunder, were heels that sidestep
cracked sidewalks (step on the crack breaks ya
momma's back)

if the breath of Black women were side steps
whoa, watch us   step

To Drown in Shug's Bathwater

Why when some of us folks want to talk about dark-
skinned Black women, we always in the overcome mode,
we been thrown aside the fitting
in and come out
as our own self
and claim our darkness.

When our images are automatically attached to
Black dark, Black nappy, vaseline dark
we some happy darkies.

Why do we come for us, plaster our names on
the statue of Black aph (afro) rodite's dark assbut strong boastful
onward-christian-sister soldiers.

How our names easily fit in the box as the
spokeskin for those purpleblackwomen?

Why is our images regally hailed as queens so dark,
cause we do know we are beautifu
in between the media low-key calling us jig-a-boos.

Or use our images as some
backward shade-ass tribute to the limitation of what is considered
Black beauty, cause none of us black women from bright
light to purple is a vision of beauty?

I thought our "you-so-Black-you-so-Blackblack" was thrown
out with Shug's bath water?

Here it comes back to roost like that Black cock,
out there fucking all the white chickens.

... And Let the Congregation Say "Let It Go"

some say blood moon's
songs are hummingbirds who
talk through girls' mouths
closed & wide open for exodus.
one way known to shake & break

afflictions of clipped-winged men—— femininity curiosity, before skin
was cut deep & her image appeared painted on clay
walls, glorified, bruised. before birth, sought her

before denial saved her. nothing's concrete
& herstory escapes adoration. in solitude
refugee blooms

purple black lilies hidden in red fields. planted
beside her bed, tossed & rippled, baptized in
the name of seclusion & the never, again. wounds
heal, just watch

a feminist oasis

her spirit is an inclusive downpour
of rain, of lightening, thunder,
harmattan winds that fly across the
middle passage whirlwinds.

her spirit spills like the calmness
swings on warm breeze
time in between summer and fall.

a sky so dark beyond black
beyond indigo, where a million stars shine.
her spirit is there, to the intangible fingers reaching
she is there too.

a disturbance in the air, the wake after waves.

it is intensified, it is noiseless, it is brash, it is loving.

she is unbalanced and she is beautiful.
she has transported before.

when her eyes close and her spirit opens
and she takes off for far off places, travels
through portals of time.

travels in the wake of her sleep.

she is made of distant places, of lakes
found in cosmic drops of blood, the
trickle of sweat between her breasts.

places that smell sweet.

silence of language when the tongue was lost
when the language was hacked, yet remained
rooted deep underneath deception.

a thousand feet beat against the earth.

she is a thousand women's calls
her tongue vibrates inside the wind
calls over the sahara.

she smells the sweet
scent of dates.

Sacred Burial Grounds

What hurt you? How you gonna heal what you can't name?
—Joy KMT

after they came and gone, she scrubs her body as though she had been
. . . reflective of a date that went wrong. when she thought to hurl her
self out the window to escape. get back to cleanliness—

pureness—as though she is far too far into life, been round too many
corners, sat on too many barstools, drunk with lust. if for that moment,
one flashback when moments, façades worn for

being in those moments. a façade that would slip, those moments she
struggled on her back or face down, tucked in her visibility. it slipped,
but she latched hold of herself and plastered it

back in place, cause this was . . . this was . . . what it was to exist in
those moments when living was merely to take up empty spaces. she
scrubs for a long minute with soap, with scented salts,

sweltering water, then bath gel, and scrubs— scrubs— scrubs. like
sandpaper, pink bath cloth tears at her skin, wipes, pain wears away
her skin, blistered, left fragile, left to heal from the erasure of their
traces.

> *her m.o. to bury skeletons of broken-messes,*
> *those jagged things buried,*
> *seep up,*
> *like underground water wells,*
> *or a woke volcano.*

her thoughts, the bowels of agitated emotions thick as spoiled milk.
emotionally she digressed—
to not have her body . . . touched. once sensual now it was like crawling
from under a fresh grave of

manure and fossilized soil. dirt glued to her skin. everywhere they
touched, their dirt took root, soiled those parts of her, those beautiful
enclaves of her body, now lay still in a grave of quicksand

and, hard to grasp her breath, as the shower's humidity roasts her throat.
but she continues to scrub, then pulls at her skin. skin cries out "i can't
help you." she yearns for gentleness, she tried to love.

last resort she tried lust. it didn't work. she—does not work, she forgets
how to caress. how to give, how to take, now, it all disgusts her. her skin
cells cannot rejuvenate fast enough to replace

herself. she has lost her way, to herself. something took flight . . . yet,
when she examines her loveliness in the mirror—it cracks a fine smile,
and stuffed inside a back pocket—its shadow.

slow dance in the basement under a red light bulb

like
 a
dance

in
 the
dark

in
 the
grind

in
 the

bent
 of backs

we un-mask.

Sankofa Blues
>*death of Jayne Cortez*

"through birth that I'm the owner from a long time ago."

She sang rouge songs.
Cheeks flushed, tongues slapped
Taste out of words that settled
Too long, afraid of truth's movement.

The poetic pulse trembles.
Her heart felt the need to pounce
Apart metaphors and call a spade,
Spade, and laugh at the kettle singing
Black, stomp the chickens that came
Home to roost.

"through birth that I'm the owner from a long time ago."

When her words were blackened,
Chained. When her words were whipped,
Unwelcomed, marked by bloodstains.

Now, poets' fingers tingle, spark,
Close to surface of bones, explode.
Words spurt out in wounded streams.
Flow in the blues, baptized
In her lullabyic poems. Tears fall,
Fears diminish, she gave
Liberation voice, freed freedom.
"from a long time ago."

>—*Jayne Cortez "Taking the Blues Back"*

Poem for My Comrades

for Dareen Tatour

poets write poems
poets are arrested   for writing poems
poets are killed   for writing poems
poets' poems incite riots
poems can be a prison bid
poems can be the executer's gun
          tried and convicted
poems forever connect Ferguson and Palestine
poems are Teflon vests for freedom fighters
poems are bedtime stories of Morrison   Hurston   Butler
poems come from God   Allah   Oshun
poems get you through the checkpoint
          or   get you caught   at the fence
poems are smuggled in book bags   in head nods
poems freed you from the darkness
          or freed you to be   the darkness
s-o-l-i-d-a-r-y   is how the word   poem   is spelled
          in some   aesthetics
poems are milk to rhetoric's tear gas
poems will wipe your tears   or bring you such torture
          tears cannot expose   that pain
poems are the yellow tape around our dead Black bodies
          black and yellow   black and blue   black and bullets
          black and dead   black and blood
poems are humorous   yeah right
a definition of poetry: "don't-have-time-for-your-shit"
the Black blood that runs underneath this country's soil
          like oil   is a liquid poem
          sticky   thick   warm   and cold like death
                    and covered in a caul

poems are your salvation
          your   temptation
                  your   lust
          your   fear
                  your   hunger
                                      poems are   thirsty
poems are the tomorrows lived before yesterday
          tomorrows that died yesterday
          but today is still   alive
poems are where taboos are open and free
          yet controlled
poems record the genocides   the bombings   the incarcerations
poems are drums   smoke signals   freed birds
poems are wrapped around telephone lines
poems are outlawed languages
          pauses inside the flesh of a poem   are ancestral languages
inside the pauses are   lost dances
          the hidden chants   the demolished memories—found poems
poems are sweat lodges
          says the poem that needs written or read or listened
          or paid attention   to
another definition of poetry: "ain't-no-signifying"
poems are nooses around   your neck
          a knife plunged into   your back
          they are a poisoned drank
one line is 1619 another 3400 BC and before the before that man
          ever knew or wants to   believe
poems write names and show asses
poems are the walking dead
poems are houses with rooms   discarded   crowded rooms
and oh yeah
          poems are full of shit   too.

Down to the River to Pray

For those who hold the secrets.

Who hold on to others' pain. Who dreams of secret places where all pain is buried. For those who believe when no one else dares to open eyes. For those who fight when no one dares to open mouths. For those who roam about the earth getting their souls dirty. For those who cannot swim well in some waters. For those who hold conversations with baobab trees. Those whose voices ride the cosmos. For those who know the sacred language of crows. For those who chase the sound of ocean waves and sit at the shores to listen to her stories. For those who birth lightening, thunder, and great storms. For those who see the beauty in unknown power. To those who rather be the storm than the petals on sunflowers.

Nights Tinker Bell Wore Combat Boots

Listen children, you too shall hear tales of Peter
& feisty Tinker Bell
who was always up in the brotha's ear.

Once, upon a midnight blue—naw bro, ebony night.
Peter exchanged his sissified dress, signifying tights
   for a restoration of
         black power independence
ass-stomping brogan boots.

Fly way cool
way fly cool

militant jacket—black leather, beret left cocked
tightrope his large bush.

Hoisted—loaded shotgun, stag-o-lee lean against right
ear—knocked Tinker hard, to the ground. Paa-Pow!

She leaped, stomped power dust from her combat boots
reshaped proudly her 10-point fro, screamed:
 death to racist pigs
high-fived her fellow fro'd, fisted sista Elaine Brown:
who promptly cleared the shit up.

Shh   listen closely to urban tales of revolutionists, sang
in ghetto patois, un-translated by COINTELPRO's
bourgeois beds
Once, upon a beautiful mother-fuckin' ebony
night, Peter & Tinker took flight under cover
of darkness, mission—to release incarcerated
militants from sleep, yo!

You still . . .

The Moon Found Her Naked

the sand said kneel, her wounded
knees sinks in its warmth and she
is swallowed in its grit. not quick,
but it roused her skin and sieved itself
into fleshy folds—a chaos-filled vessel.

     the grains gathered in her
     desolation.

her body of trauma, of memories buried
in prayers of the desert's sands and her
breath, heavy recoils from recalls.

there may be no sound, but she is a
humming moan. it is the song that
drifts when the wind dives into the
dunes. a tickle of sand particles rides
the winds of the west harmattan
—what sound could this be?

a dance of saharan dust travels as far
as the caribbean, florida, the gulf coast,
& northward sirocco winds rocks her bed.

on it fly silverbills and black-
face firefinches.

spreads like snow in the desert, she
lays her body on this earthen & fire
from her pores, drips.

     her flesh seeps moistness
     that drenches & cools her.

& the lion appears, fondles her, & both
weep as the moon catches her nakedness.

These Dreams Beaten and Battered

You know, I stopped
living   decades ago.
No pinpoints that tack
the morning's reflection
in the full-length mirror.
No telltale snitch of when
the vagina's anchor dropped,
it just   stopped.

Soft like snowflakes
wind surfs on air, lands
on your eyelashes, beautiful
skeletons, catcher of dreams
then melts and blurs your
way, like that—I—stopped
living.

No gather
of belly-fatten women
or over-stuff toppled
signs, smell of a burnt
stainless and steel pot
on the stove, when water
evaporates—and—you are
too busy, or already full
of forgets.

As the sun draws down
or you dance to music in
your head, it feels distant
feels false, cause when did
you dance? When did you
ever hit those high notes?
Yet

you remember as the smoke
alarms buzz, and you reach to
hit the hard plastic with the
handle of a wood broom cause
nothing's been on fire, in your
house, for a—while.

Agitation

Search for it—not the touch of a woman
But—womanist touch. The known art
Why we do—did, done for . . . Why we
Spar so hard, not to do what's required
To do out of spite. Of no reason, no
Legalist's rhyme. We just want to let go.
Still, we search for us—we tied up in
False blush. Lipstick draws our lips thin
Crusted pencil lead has filled a journal of
Questions. Rebuttals jello, jiggle when
We scamper in our light—doing our thang.

Twilight on Kool Darkness

Variables curtsy
Behind the swang
Duchess voice
		di—she—wahhhh.
Tongu manipulates
Gush of air, scat
Wings retreat
		do-be-do-bap-di-she-wah.
Keel as drumsticks fall
Against skin, tender
Sassy whisks
		skeep-beep de bop-bop.
Etched sand glass landscape
Or gives a damn
Melody
		be-dope skeetle-at-op-de-day.
Bellowing blue notes
Chicago damn
Sax o' heart
		oohh bop sha bam
Shake rhythm beneath
Blues lady's scats.
Off-beat hearts
		bop-bee-shaaa.
Burst hummingbird's throat
Night gale's air chill
Ricochets off
		bo-bee-shaaa.
Cheeks, delicate its
Dimpled sound sinks
Cuts in spurts
		ooh bop sha bam.
Quiet flight, quiet
Butterfly, flight
Empty space
		di-she-wahhhh.
Lady's fingers dap
When voices go
Silently blues.

Why Should They Care?
after to Jessica Care Moore

wired to transmit
mittens not kid
gloves, not bare of
threads weaved tight
quilted, welded
melted gold, since
her words did not
fit, not warrant
life beyond queued
   debatable
hate-able quotes
bounce off air as
rubber & glue
wired to re-
decorate minds
tinged heart whores
stuck awarded
pages define
lairs located
in daily queues
incorrect acts
who be dat, who
dat be, be who
wired to transmit
not kid gloves here
lips disjointed
mouths just hangout
no walls for flies
unhinged flung text
splat like mud pies
   invisible
against those ghost
surrogate lies

tied knotted, full
bodied bloodied
names sang in hulls
reeked of death, life-
less corpses, hung
strung one against
one, back-to-back
tribe-to-tribe, tongues
names whispered,
spoke *yɛ were ha:*
here we are, listen
dash-dot-dash-dash
free of coded
layered lies, inked
bewitched stories
lies fitted flat
against bare breast
breastfed fables
draped onion skins
drippy dicks weep
lay weakened as
black skin steppin
fetchin post-race
empty words, gun
play in black backs
witness blind-bind
traitors, haters,
border babies
lost, lost, lost, lost.
thank God for words
not fitting, don't
care, dare if you
must. ever since

thoughts machete dug
deep through do-do
race sings sinful
loudly, cause it
don't care, no need
to care, truth runs
fast, free, funky
truth plays outside
after bedtime
runs in streets, runs
against traffic
bare foot, bare head
prints, imprints run
silent: we are here.

Middle Passage Speed Bump

Copulation of 300 thousand-year-old sperm, damaged eggs, gave
birth to a nation. Once submerged as an endangered species of coral,
skeletal bones, fractioned, partially buried in ocean sand, polished
generations, crush undercurrents, left triangular path, nourished
footprints, sodden blood laminations, mummified under ocean,
sand, fragmented whole bodies unwashed, made up four million-
death, 400-years of labor, birth of nation, we sold each other, for
scholarly acceptance. Released shackled, people, of these we march-

Do As I Do, *wait,* Do As I Say

Folks share, Instagram party vines, drunk cats, hotmess dj'ing ghetto
mix, selfish selfies, folks giving, not- not free breakfast lines. Pokes,
likes bomb social hoods, drones bomb Gaza; drones get closer to us
/US, via Amazon. Me-occupied games, fingers grope screens. Hand
games, clap slap, clap slap

meanwhile monkey got choked, New, New, York. There is enough
to spray around. Canisters body surf jeering crowds. It is not over.
On? It is going. Share it. Free falling Ferguson. Blackflip out of sight
(out-of-mind). Long time dead bodies, ignite. Black-out, media led
regression. Palms up, clap slap

Palms up down. Freed of gun (can of soda); gun (skittles); gun (driver's
license). Up hold, hold up. Hot, Black skin. Not, cause it pops in clubs.
Grinds on stage. Too cool in painted house. Foolish fools. Protection
covered sun. Ain't true. Now skin needs gun-screen. Get ready. Here
it comes. Its gots to come, human

rights. When military turns up. When they tattoo your ass, messy lives
if we do not find a way; stop this madness-marches. Candles/stuffed
bears- not again. It is gonna be- Soweto; gonna be- Red Cliff Indian
Reservation; gonna be- segregation's, gentrification's by-product.
Every sidewalk crack a Black foot

sidestep via Ferguson, New York, Pittsburgh, Oakland. Delivers blows
via new legal poachers- police, givers of excessive trickery, it is going
on, it's going. . .

Got to Get Away

ọkan:
each day's step board a train, red-eyed plane
megabus to lose—self. desert—self, surround
self—with nothingness. at times—all this mess
needs to shut down, get the fuck out of town
cause i, too—liked it better when we stood
our ground, when we had ground, when pimps
walked, side cocked hats, floppy, plaid, wide
bottom belled. button down polyester exposed
chest hairs (god forbid brown skins seek out
polyester-too day). i, too, liked it better when
black was always trippin; negroes couldn't walk
reject squared dances, hips' move that slop stalk
tighten-up, dip-it, slide-it moves. "stop swanging
them hips," momma's shout to sassa-frassy
daughters—like mothers, like daughters, like
the beats drag on, lps play long, they so cool
i listen & pretend one day i'd be hippy kool.

meji:
took me landside far, ran me through mother
father, way back grands moms, dads, way
back to mammy's slaved titties, massa tilling
dicks, slave bucks. wretched me back to ships
dark, dank stank places where shit, chants, &
prayers fed babylon's mixed cesspool.

mẹta:
damned shoulders of a thomas, burdened lovers
heavy you carry on, take it higher, keep it all
the way live, scribes baraka, knight, & them
dudes. if i had any tears left—"d cry cause
gotta be hope in this—fucked-up place.

mẹrin:
stand ground, the ladies sang, ain't ground
beneath our feet they wail, they take us back
to when real black was dashiki. no imitation
amazon droned delivered. big ass 'fros, hot
pants. when no one tried to be black, but us
cause being us was too complicated, komplex.
they take us back to mecca. before ghost riders
trampled african ground, to any americas
mixing got us all mongrelized. she sweetly
guides us back to those lands, land when
we—us, before blood was tainted with blood.

marun:
life was better, we lived out loud—black
we knew "turncoats." we knew male
we knew female, we knew love, hate
we knew addicts, drunks, we knew all this
we knew "us." we neva lost us, we had back
up—black dudes back there, were black, big
ass 'fros, dukee cornrows, laughing, hands
back black slapping, it was a blessing to be.

mẹfa:
still—we stood our ground, momentarily rocks
crackled, all fucked up, uniformly informed
"sleeper" po-pos bout to fuck us all up. zombied
militarization mode. stand down, coward stance
cause tag—you're it. black folks scared of losing
whatever esteem degrees achieved, post-better
blue, people of color, think it's gonna save them
when it comes down to the black, no—it's class
vs. money. save us, ain't nothing gonna, but . . .

Blackmania, Peoples oof Color Random—Mess #1

DNA ninety-nine-dollar test, given out of gold cadillac
trunks wrapped in paper promises. promises to reveal nappily
ever after roots, to find your origins buried in shea butter,
coconut oil, and as the drummed definition of ethnicity's
inaccuracy floats to the top:
of whom you might have been, could have been
who they took from you, burnt from you,
hung from you, raped of wombs, whipped from you.
you. the you stolen from your mothers, stolen from your fathers,
your lands stolen, your languages cut from your tongues,
your stolen history. Your stolen DNA—sold back to you.

The Reckoning

today the learning and the breaking becomes another hashtag. appropriation. but folks eat it up like it is 100%. today the wanting to cite african in america history, before, would never admit to reading, liking, any amiri baraka poem, some even the flaming tongue of james baldwin was only whispered in closed rooms. or poets who have names but are stifled, or poets who have been cancelled but their words echo still. or still too afraid to say the word motherfucker, but love to whip the words bitch, shit, pussy, and dick. for those who follow toasted sesame seed breadcrumbs into the darkness, but not into the dark darkness, but only to the line where the light is dim, but still lit enough to see the safety of its dawn. cause to stand in darkness is still too much a real revolution and they still not ready to break free or call a motherfucker, cause they want to write to teach to be part of those other somethings. or those who been black since birth, now admitting, their hair is nappy, or straight-up they did not wake up like this, cause it is relaxed. we always confuse about what is and what is not acceptable black or woke or black or woke or black or to be a human being. some want to fit in all the spaces. heck all these hips and ass is too big for most spaces, and so i take up comfortably large spaces everywhere my black ass goes, and it is the heavy hips that balance this earth. rock on sistas. smile and, *put your hands on your hips and let your backbone slip.* let the world fall and find its own way out of its darkness. cause we about to walk out this motherfucker into the light.

Acknowledgment

Poems previously published:

Every Morning a Foot is Looking for my Neck (chapbook)
Central Square Press
Being a Single Black Woman on a Moonlit Night (When
Lightning Rides Thunder Bareback)
Every morning a Foot is Looking for my Neck
When the Walls Close in

Where We Stand, Poems of Black Resilience Anthology
The Eleventh Hour Manifesto
A Political Act, Absolutely

Taint Taint Taint Literary Magazine
Death Doula's Song

The Massachusetts Review
Twilight on Kool Darkness

Solstice a Magazine of Diverse Voices
Nina's Fire: Frantic's Go-Go

Hot Metal Bridge Journal
Rosary Prayers

JoINT. Literary Magazine
Public notice: women next

Thank you to those poets of the Black Arts Movement—my first mentors. To the poets I have had the opportunity to share a mic, who have inspired me with their own words. Being in the room with other poets has allowed me to continue this poetic evolution.

To Get Fresh Publishers for this platform, and to the editors who pointed out the extra "s" as my dialect moved from mouth to page, confirming we write in our language.

The poems in this book were inspired by a constant search for self-identity through the private conversations within my DNA, the sound of ocean currents and waves, the echo of thunder and lightning, and the whisper of prayers and healing chants.

Most importantly, I thank my daughters Winter, Simone, and Venezuela, who are my rock and encouragers. To my family, friends, and community of poet friends as we acknowledge and support each other. Thank you, Mom, for your love.

Bonita Lee Penn, is a Pittsburgh poet, editor, curator and author of the chapbook, *Every Morning a Foot Is Looking For My Neck* (Central Square Press, 2019). She is a recipient of the 2023 Advancing Black Arts in Pittsburgh grant to produce her poetic stage project, "Gospel in the Wake.' Her work has appeared in the award-winning anthology *Where We Stand: Poems of Black Resilience,* and in *JOINT.Literary Magazine, Hot Metal Bridge Journal, The Massachusetts Review, "The Skinny" Poetry Journal, Women Studies Quarterly, Voices from the Attic Anthology.*

She serves on the Sweetwater Center for Arts Board of Directors and Managing Editor, Soul Pitt Quarterly Magazine. Penn is also a Martha's Vineyard Institute of Creative Writing Fellow; member of the performance band Heroes Are Gang Leaders, poetry facilitator for Madwomen in the Attic, and the United Black Book Clubs of Pittsburgh, Founder of B's Bags, LLC, and member of ASALH (Association for the Study of African American Life and History).